Applied Theosophy

Also in this series:

Theosophy and the Search for Happiness
Texts by Moon Laramie and Annie Besant

Art and Theosophy
Texts by Martin Firrell and A.L. Pogosky

Theosophy and Esoteric Christianity
*Texts by Isis Resende, R. Heber Newton
& Franz Hartmann*

Theosophy and Yoga
Texts by Jenny Baker and Annie Besant

Theosophy and Social Justice
*Texts by Dr. Barbara B. Hebert, William Quan Judge
& Annie Besant*

The Purpose of Theosophy
Texts by Petra Meyer & Patience Sinnett

Theosophy and the Conscious Mind
Texts by Pablo Sender & H.P. Blavatsky

Anne Kelly

Anne Kelly was born in California, USA and has been living in the south-west of the United Kingdom since 2009. She has a background in public speaking and has been an on-air radio and television presenter for 30 years. She has voiced thousands of commercials, did stand up comedy for a short while and was a tour guide at Universal Studios. Since 2002, Anne has also been a lecturer and motivational speaker on confidence building, communication and overcoming addiction.

As a labour of love, and to be of service to humanity, she began voicing theosophical texts anonymously under the name Living Theosophy. The texts she shared included *The Key to Theosophy*, *Light on the Path* and *The Voice of the Silence*. She hosted book studies, interviewed other theosophists and shared her own experience of these ancient teachings across global social media platforms.

Anne is a Trustee of the Theosophical Society in Scotland, a member of Blavatsky Lodge, London and works in media broadcasting for the Theosophical Society in England.

In 2016, she launched Yogi Philosophy Publications to republish, and create audio books of, three theosophical classics, *The Voice of the Silence*, *Light on the Path* and *The Fourteen Lessons in Yogi Philosophy and Oriental Occultism*.

Anne is a dedicated student of theosophy and hosts the Living Theosophy YouTube channel, devoted to spreading the theosophical message around the world.

Applied Theosophy
by Anne Kelly (2021)

The theme of theosophy in practical application is an important one. Though the teachings of theosophy originated in antiquity, they are meant to be lived and applied in the world of today, the third millennium. The teachings are there to be discovered and to enable us to remember who we truly are as human beings. From the most ancient writings known to man, these teachings underpin all of the world's religions, sciences and philosophies. The time to access the teachings is now. There is no more important task. We must work to overcome the limitations of our selves and understand our connection to each other. We must learn to stop destroying our planet and understand that attempting to rule over each other through brute force is not the answer.

We can learn a lot from the Christmas Truce of 1914. Young German, French and British soldiers, huddled deep in icy, muddy trenches, experienced a brief Christmas Eve respite from the conflict of World War One. They had spent every day fighting battles instigated by old men far away. To lift their spirits, soldiers sang Christmas carols and called out amicably to their 'enemies' across No

Man's Land, the narrow expanse between the trenches.

Eventually, a German soldier shouted out, 'Tomorrow, you no shoot, we no shoot.' Over Christmas Day and most of Boxing Day, they mingled, took photos, shared champagne, cigarettes, laughter and their hopes to end the war between their countries as soon as possible. Some of the men even shared a friendly football game, though no one knew where the ball came from. Not all soldiers took part in the truce. Some even opened fire on those who were participating in this extraordinary event. But the participants were those who were able to see something of themselves in their so-called enemies. With camaraderie, empathy and love, they acted in a spirit of shared humanity. They became one, they were each other. Christmas, our modern celebration of the birth of 'Christ' or rather 'Christos' - the divine spirit in every human - was the setting for this 'Christmas truce,' during a brutal war. Often denied or doubted through the years, this moment remains a powerful inspiration for mankind today, for it was truly theosophy in action.

George Arundale writes, 'Theosophy is

suggested to be a Wisdom even more ancient than the religions, even though it appears to us today with a Greek label.'[1]

He goes on, 'Theosophy is no dogma. It is no formal religion. It is no specific mode of science. It is no carefully constructed philosophy representing the gaze of man into the heavens. It is an Experience of Reality on the part of some who, transcending the microcosm, have become in a measure free in the macrocosm, and describe something of their vision of the infinite as reflected in, and in terms of, the finite.'[2]

We must know who we truly are. What is our purpose? Why are we here? What comes next beyond this physical life? And how can we help when there is so much suffering in the world? The sages of the past have lovingly advised us: 'Man know thyself, then thou shalt know the Universe and God.' We have attributed this quote variously to Pythagoras, Socrates and the Oracle at Delphi but what does it truly mean? It is only through courageous yet humble and diligent self-analysis that we can understand what we genuinely are. Above all else, our self-reflection and search for truth must be selfless.

Luke 17: 20-21: 'The kingdom of God is not coming in ways that can be observed, nor will they say, 'Look, here it is!' or 'There!' for behold, the kingdom of God is in the midst of you.'

Midst means 'in the middle of', not a separate being within a crowd surrounding you, but literally inside of you. It is within all of us and inside every thing.

'*Know ye not that ye are the temple of God, and that the spirit of (the absolute) God dwelleth in you?* Yet, let no man anthropomorphise that essence in us. Let no theosophist, if he would hold to divine, not human truth, say that this 'God in secret' listens to, or is distinct from, either finite man or the infinite essence - for all are one.'[3]

Somewhere, somehow this essential message has become confused and lost. Sadly, we continue to look for salvation outside ourselves rather than taking personal responsibility, which makes us as powerless as leaves blowing in the wind.

When we begin to look inward, we recognise that ancient sacred texts do not describe an anthropomorphic 'God' that comes from a separate realm. God does not have human characteristics like insecurity and rage. God does not punish the ignorant with an eternity of deathless torment. The sacred texts, through analogy, parable and mythology, refer to our internal 'higher selves' as 'god' and our lower selves as 'man'. In the *Bhagavad Gita*, we understand that Krishna is the higher self conversing with Arjuna, the lower self.

To differentiate between my own higher and lower selves, I find it helpful to refer to the age-old virtues of man. Here virtue is defined as 'good moral character': humility not pride; kindness not envy; temperance not gluttony; chastity not lust; patience not anger; charity/liberality not greed; and diligence not sloth.

> *'The enemies which rise within the body,*
> *Hard to be overcome - the evil passions -*
> *Should manfully be fought, who conquers these*
> *Is equal to the conqueror of worlds'.*[4]

We are advised to 'first deserve, then desire.' As we follow the path of life, each one of us develops at our own pace. We find that the purer the vessel, the easier the access to truth.

When I reached certain milestones on my own journey, I dubbed the experience, 'the falling away'. I was born an empath and, like so many others, I had a childhood that was difficult and painful. It included experiences of abandonment, betrayal and rejection. As I grew up, I frequently found myself in unhealthy, co-dependent relationships with plenty of excuses to self-medicate and self-destruct. I understand now that I was battling an insatiable desire to fill the emptiness inside me with temporary, earthly solutions. I would do anything to numb the mind and gain a brief reprieve from my psychological suffering. My selfish actions made circumstances exponentially worse for both me and others. I have found that many who drink and do drugs are simply looking to change the way they feel. They are clutching at a fleeting euphoria or, more often than not, they hope to feel nothing at all.

Some people can partake and even enjoy a moderate amount of these substances. For many, wine is a 'food'. But not for me. The romantic ideal of a candlelit dinner accompanied by a glass of wine soon became a portal to hell - with a few stops at the police station, jail, and the local mental ward on the way down. Thank God I stopped when I did and that the damage was moderate. I am so very grateful that no one was injured or killed. My heart breaks for the others who have far more devastating stories to tell. I am no different from them. I was just lucky enough to pull the throttle back a little earlier.

Sometimes it takes an agonising and humiliating faceplant from great heights to truly shake one awake. When we drink to numb pain, we end up a slave, endlessly feeding the 'hungry ghost' until we become a ghost ourselves. Like the torments of Tantalus, we never get to taste what we truly desire: love, acceptance, purpose, hope, calm, understanding, truth. What a revelation it will be when we finally understand that our search must ultimately lead to what has been inside us all along, closer than our own breath. My experience has revealed that progress on the path of life remains limited until we have made our vessels - our bodies - pure and deserving.

In her *Collected Writings* HPB says, 'No animal food of whatever kind, nothing that has life in it, should be taken by the disciple. No wine, no spirits, or opium should be used: for these are like the Lhamayin (evil spirits) who fasten upon the unwary, they devour the understanding.'[5]

To those who have never experienced the haunting throes of addiction, I frequently point toward a common horror movie theme; demonic possession. You feel locked inside your self with a darkness that fights for control, a darkness that can only be 'exorcised' by you from within. This work cannot be done by anything exterior nor can the darkness be cast out via any ceremony, religious or otherwise.

Blavatsky also wrote, 'Alcohol in all its forms has a direct, marked, and very deleterious influence on man's psychic condition. Wine and spirit drinking is only less destructive to the development of the inner powers, than the habitual use of hashish, opium, and similar drugs.'[6] The use of alcohol, she says, has a 'directly pernicious action upon the brain',[7] particularly the pineal and pituitary glands. Alcohol prevents the development of the 'third eye'. In *The Fourteen Lessons in Yogi Philosophy and Oriental Occultism*, William Walker Atkinson described bars and pubs where undeveloped souls 'hang around the scenes of their old degrading lives, and often take possession of the brain of one of their own kind, who may be under the influence of liquor, and thus add to his own low desires'.[8]

***

My husband and I were separated. We shared custody of our son Alex. An opportunity presented itself to me offering much needed love and stability - the chance to move from California to the English countryside. I thought this move would also be fantastic for my child. I soon learned that there are no winners in a child custody 'battle'. A fair visitation schedule had been put in place despite the distances involved. I was not expecting any resistance to the move. I sincerely believed I was doing the best for our son. But equally, Alex's father thought he was doing the right thing in opposing the move from the US to the UK.

Alex was in England for a year and flourished. However, frequent international travel is tough for a child. He would also return from visits to California distressed by his parents' venomous 'war'.

I realised that he could not continue to live this way and that the ultimate victory in any custody case is to provide two peaceful, loving parents no matter the child's physical location. I realised one of us would have to surrender and step off the battlefield, and it was not going to be Alex's father. For me to live without Alex was completely heartbreaking. I would rather have burned at the stake. But how to truly teach him about compassion unless I put it into practice myself?

Letting go of my only child, the one thing I cherished above all else, and the excruciating pain that followed, ushered in my life's most beautiful treasure - the discovery of theosophy.

'Do not be afraid of your difficulties. Do not wish you could be in other circumstances than you are. For when you have made the best of an adversity, it becomes the stepping stone to a splendid opportunity.'[9]

It is true that heartache can pave the way for wisdom. In the grief of living a world away from my son, feeling I had nothing more to lose, I turned to a forgotten little book I had picked up years before. I had stopped to pick up some sandalwood incense at a metaphysical bookshop called The Bodhi Tree in Santa Monica, California. The book I found there had a long but interesting title: *The Fourteen Lessons in Yogi Philosophy and Oriental Occultism*. It was written by William Walker Atkinson under the nom de plume Yogi Ramacharaka.

I had spent my early years in Catholic school. I had gone on to explore the complexities of the New Age movement, finding only glimmers of inspiration. Now this century-old text seemed to vibrate with truth! I returned to read it again and again. Its lessons pointed me to the classic theosophical text *Light on the Path* by Mabel Collins. I developed a thirst for theosophy. I soon found myself at the Theosophical Society in London. In my mind I was absolutely certain the building would be full of people. I envisioned floors full of busy, happy people. I was shocked to see such quiet and emptiness. Sadly, hundreds of texts containing the ancient wisdoms sat locked behind library doors. I signed up as a member enthusiastically and was delighted to enrol on the first study course. Deep joy took hold within when I realised *The Fourteen Lessons in Yogi Philosophy and Oriental Occultism* was actually a summary of theosophical teachings and the study course allowed me to explore them in depth. This journey of discovery was like a quest, an exploration of my own little *DaVinci Code*.

I expected a healthy roster of students and was disappointed to see only four at the first class. They seemed to have a good working knowledge of theosophy but I found myself leaving each session with more questions than answers.

The classes dwindled down to just me and my two tutors, but this only increased my appetite to learn. I went on to study with any online theosophical groups I could find and I desperately wished to be of service somehow. As a former radio and television broadcaster, I didn't know what else to do but make audio versions of theosophical texts and upload them to YouTube. Once digitised, I trusted that they would find their way to wherever in the world they needed to be. I kept at it and uploaded *The Fourteen Lessons…* chapter by chapter, then I added *Light on the Path*, *The Voice of the Silence* and began hosting book study videos of *The Key to Theosophy*. I also shared my own experiences of applying this essential knowledge.

In truth, I didn't feel qualified. But equally, I didn't see anyone else doing this work and I felt instinctively that it must be done. I chose the name *Living Theosophy* as it is my belief that there is nothing more important to do. I would gladly use my last breath to proclaim, 'Live theosophy! Become it!'

'Theosophy is who theosophy does, not thinks, not studies, not feels but does.'[10]

This is not a journey for the ego, nor do I believe it to be an academic journey either. There is something quite magical, purposeful, healing and true that takes place when the theosophical teachings are put into practice in our day-to-day lives.

It is my understanding that the ageless wisdom of theosophy is literally a textbook for humanity and, when applied in every day life, it helps us navigate our time here on earth. Theosophy offers substantial, factual answers to every question imaginable. We find purpose and ways to cope in life with equanimity, focus and a sense of long-lost understanding. Finally, the solutions to life's problems are available. We are encouraged to study and compare every religion, science and philosophy, to look for, and identify, the similarities. Within these commonalities, we come to recognise the glowing embers of pure theosophy.

Shortly after my journey began, I became vegetarian, which was relatively easy to do given the brilliant meat substitutes available now. I was influenced by the loving nature of those around me and I wished to change my diet solely for ethical reasons. Meals still contained dairy products and that meant that cheese was an essential. Also oils and breads were regular staples. I quickly put on quite a bit of weight but given the state of my emotions, I didn't really notice nor was I much bothered - I was absorbed with what was taking place within. This disengagement allowed my physical appearance to become quite matronly. Every day, I wore long black flowing clothes from head to toe and my hair in a messy knot. I wore no makeup and was far more focused on comfort and functionality than fashion. The move to England and living away from Alex had such a powerful impact, I even adopted long-term celibacy while I nurtured my maternal broken heart. When not behind the desk in my studio, long walks in the English countryside with theosophical texts on robotic 'read back' from Kindle were the norm.

In the spring of 2018, I realised dairy products should be solely for the animals they were intended. I finally grasped that cheese and milk were not acceptable in my diet. I could no longer sustain my body with the products of other beings' suffering. We have so much to learn from the animal kingdom - they live in the moment, love without condition, only take what they need. They do not worry nor do they judge. Humans are absurdly cruel to animals, yet we share this planet. One day we will look back and want to beg their forgiveness for the horrors we have inflicted.

I chose to be vegan solely for compassionate reasons, but to my surprise, my body benefitted and began to heal itself. I was no longer bloated with a bluish hue to my skin. The extra weight came off quickly and without effort. I suddenly had a ridiculous amount of energy. My blood pressure went down, skin, hair and eyes brightened, and I came to life as never before.

Now sober and vegan, I embraced what I had

been looking for all along - the ancient teachings of theosophy. It feels as if I have found the Holy Grail itself. The grail is not a physical object but a process that takes place here in the physical world when this ancient knowledge is put into practical application. All of the work takes place within. We look towards our inner ladder, the antahkarana, and gratefully grasp its mystical rungs. Step by step, we rise above our earthy personality with all of its undesirable characteristics. Our job is to overcome our lower selves, climbing ever higher and understanding that all spiritual development takes place inside of us. This is the great challenge.

The term *theosophy* is thousands of years old. It is not a religion nor is it a church. *There is no religion higher than truth* is the motto of the Theosophical Society. Theosophy is the ancient divine wisdom incorporating sacred science and divine knowledge. It is divine math and quantum physics. It is universal ethics and compassion for all life, the timeless unity and love taught by every sage and avatar throughout the ages. It serves as a signpost for humanity to look toward the kingdom of heaven within. As each one of us evolves, through self-reflection and self-realisation, we understand that we are the temple and we look to nature as the true church.

Today, the holiness of nature is being recognised more and more. In a recent interview on CNN, Prince Charles said, 'Nature herself has her own rights, and we have a responsibility to try to remember that. And there are, I've always felt, sacred aspects in all this, which… the more we desacralise nature, the worse it gets.' Nature is the ultimate divinity. Let us work in harmony with her.

When asked what theosophy is, I explain, to the best of my understanding, that it is the ageless wisdom, based on fact not faith. Theosophy can be traced back through recorded history to its ancient roots. The sacred embers of this timeless truth shine through in the commonalities of the world's religions, sciences and philosophies. It is not exclusive but inclusive. Parallel wisdoms can be seen in Esoteric Buddhism, the Kabbalah, alchemy, the works of Pythagoras, Plato, and Paracelsus, as well as in Alexandrian Philosophy, the Bhagavad Gita, the Dao, the Vedas, the Upanishads, the writings of the Sufi poet Rumi, Native American spirituality,

Hermeticism, the works of Jakob Bohme, in Freemasonry, in the work of 20th-century philosopher Manly P. Hall and many more. These sacred mysteries have been respected in the great antediluvian civilisations of Egypt, China, Greece and India. Theosophy belongs to all and solely to none. It cannot be taught nor bought, but it can be earned and learned. It is to be lived, not simply read, studied or pontificated about.

In *The Secret Doctrine* Blavatsky writes, 'That it (theosophy) is the uninterrupted record covering thousands of generations of Seers whose respective experiences were made to test and to verify the traditions passed orally by one early race to another, of the teachings of higher and exalted beings, who watched over the childhood of Humanity. That for long ages, the ' Wise Men ' of the Fifth Race, of the stock saved and rescued from the last cataclysm and shifting of continents, had passed their lives in learning, not teaching.

'How did they do so? It is answered: by checking, testing, and verifying in every department of nature the traditions of old by the independent visions of great adepts; i.e., men who have developed and perfected their physical, mental, psychic, and spiritual organisations to the utmost possible degree. No vision of one adept was accepted till it was checked and confirmed by the visions - so obtained as to stand as independent evidence - of other adepts, and by centuries of experiences.'[11]

We, too, cannot know anything until it is put into practice and we experience the results for ourselves. Just as a scientist proves a theory through a physical experiment, we must verify our understanding through personal experience.

Earth is at a critical time in its evolution. Many empaths are incarnating, each with a feeling of responsibility for, and close connection with, all beings and with nature. In my understanding, this is inherently theosophical. These deep thinking, deep feeling empaths offer much hope for humanity as they embody the understanding that all and everything is one.

Many empathetic souls feel they should work to change the world. Yet the only way this can be done is to change our own thoughts, our own behaviours, our own actions and reactions. Simply put, we must change ourselves.

We have been conditioned to look for the solution outside of ourselves, Many people still expect a 'saviour' to come and rescue us. But this is simply giving our power away. Nothing and nobody can save us, except ourselves. There are still many millions awaiting some kind of supernatural figure to swoop down from the sky and rescue the 'chosen few'. Because of their lust for power and control, religious institutions have brainwashed us into believing that spiritual enlightenment can only be doled out by the elite and the ordained. They reinforce the idea that our salvation lies in the external, beyond our own consciousness. Before the universal principles were written down, they were preserved orally in myths and folklore. We, ourselves, are the heroes we have been looking for.

On Heroes, Myth and Marvel

'Mythology is the repository of man's most ancient science, and what concerns us chiefly is this - when truly interpreted once more, it is destined to be the death of those false theologies to which it has unwittingly given birth.' And 'Ancient mythology...

Its fables were the means of conveying facts; they were neither forgeries nor fictions.'[12]

Through the millennia, the metaphors of our myths and legends have provided an essential operator's manual for mankind. Never to be taken literally, they include intricate symbolism to illustrate truth. We can recognise both the hero and the villain within ourselves: the hero, our higher self; the villain, our earthly lower self. Mythological quests comprise daunting adventures with trials, bloody battles and woe, but also triumph, success and, often, wise and loving assistance. Myths illuminate not only our planetary and spiritual journey but also offer lessons on ethics, the laws of nature, the keys to the mysteries, the universe, philosophy, science and the union of mortals and gods.

Here in 2021, Disney's Marvel Comic movie franchise continues to produce a multitude of superheroes, providing similar storylines around the eternal battle between 'good and evil'. Their heroes most often save the day with 'other worldly' physical strength through individual personality rather than calling upon the divine spark within. The extraordinary CGI special effects of might and muscle surely sell more tickets, and tap into the very human traits of competition, power and the desire for exclusive special powers. But every man is more than man and when we discover who we truly are, the evolution to 'superhuman' becomes possible and real.

'The Universe is worked and guided from within outwards. As above so it is below, as in heaven so on earth ; and man - the microcosm and miniature copy of the macrocosm - is the living witness to this Universal Law and to the mode of its action.'[13]

In *The Key to Theosophy*, the third object of the Theosophical Society is given as follows: 'To investigate the hidden mysteries of Nature under every aspect possible, and the psychic and spiritual powers latent in man especially.'[14] Latent, meaning 'existing but concealed'. We have far more potential than the limits suggested by our five senses. With the state of our planet as it is, there is literally no time to waste. Our emotions are the 'engine' and our thoughts, the 'rudder'. Let us then take back the wheel and access our 'kingdom of heaven' within. It is time we consciously navigate through life rather than being arbitrarily blown about by the four winds.

The law of attraction is a mighty, life-changing truth that is far too valuable to paraphrase. From *The Secret Doctrine Volume II*: 'It was by Kriyasakti, that mysterious and divine power latent in the will of every man, and which, if not called to life, quickened and developed by Yogi-training, remains dormant in 999,999 men out of a million, and gets atrophied.'

'Kriyasakti' - the mysterious power of thought which enables it to produce external, perceptible, phenomenal results by its own inherent energy. The ancients held that any idea will manifest itself externally, if one's attention (and Will) is deeply concentrated upon it ; similarly, an intense volition will be followed by the desired result.'[15]

HPB writes in *The Theosophical Glossary* that 'Kriyasakti' is the power of thought; one of the seven forces of nature. Creative potency of the Siddhis (powers) of the full Yogis.'[16]

Raghavan Iyer has written that one must have '…an unshakeable conviction of the inherent value of the action of Kriyashakti, independent of entropy and of the reflection of creativity in the complex processes of change. It is the unbroken assurance of the Divine, which is unborn and undying; it is the full freedom of selflessness, the formless joy and boundless beneficence that gives freely of itself without a shadow or hint of calculation. Thus, the allegorical offspring of Dharma and Shraddha is the mystical power of divine creation at the heart of the invisible cosmos. It is Kriyasakti personified as Kamadeva, the infinite potency of Divine Thought and the Law of laws, Compassion Absolute.'[17]

'Kriyasakti… This faculty, creative in its effects, is so, simply because it is the active agent of that attribute on the objective plane. Like the lightning conductor which leads the electric fluid, the faculty of Kriyasakti conducts the creative quintessence and gives it direction. Led haphazardly, it can kill; directed by the human intellect, it can create according to a predetermined plan.

'When in the course of ages nations developed, which in their egotism and ferocious vanity were convinced of their complete superiority to all others, past or present, when the development of Kriyasakti became more and more difficult and the divine faculty had almost disappeared from the earth, they forgot little by little the science of their earlier ancestors. They even went further and rejected altogether the tradition of their antediluvian parents, denying with contempt the presence of a spirit and a soul in this, the most ancient of all sciences. Of the three great attributes of nature, they only accepted the existence of matter or rather its illusory aspect, for of real matter or substance even the materialists themselves confess a complete ignorance; and truly they have never caught the slightest glimpse of it, not even from afar. Thus came to birth modern Chemistry.'[18]

The Law of Attraction has been substantially diluted and commercialised to appeal to mankind's greed and materialism. However, it remains a powerful law that can transform our lives. In 1908, William Walker Atkinson, deeply inspired by fellow theosophist and animal/women's rights campaigner Anna Kingsford and mystical author Edward Maitland, wrote *The Kybalion*. This is a short but powerful text on the Hermetic Philosophy of ancient Egypt and Greece. *The Kybalion* was published under the pen name The Three Initiates, this titanic little book has paved the way to theosophy for many.

'…The Hermetists teach that the great work of influencing one's environment is accomplished by Mental Power. The Universe being wholly mental, it follows that it may be ruled only by Mentality. And in this truth is to be found an explanation of all the phenomena and manifestations of the various mental powers which are attracting so much attention and study in these earlier years of the Twentieth Century. Back of and under the teachings of the various cults and schools, remains ever constant the principle of the Mental Substance of the Universe. If the Universe be Mental in its substantial nature, then it follows that Mental Transmutation must change the conditions and phenomena of the Universe. If the Universe is Mental, then Mind must be the highest power affecting its phenomena. If this be understood then all the so-called 'miracles' and 'wonder-workings' are seen plainly for what they are. The All is Mind; The Universe is Mental.'[19]

It was seeing this law explained in *Isis Unveiled* that enabled me to put it into practice at last. I was finally able to change a long pattern of painful, negative thinking. By working to rid myself of a particularly obsessive thought pattern, I successfully changed the nature of the circumstances I attracted to myself. I finally found that I do, indeed, have control over my thoughts and emotions. Everyone one of us does. This phenomenal process changed my life.

'As God creates, so man can create. Given a certain intensity of will, and the shapes created by the mind become subjective. Hallucinations, they are called, although to their creator they are real as any visible object is to any one else. Given a more intense and intelligent concentration of this will, and the form becomes concrete, visible, objective; the man has learned the secret of secrets; he is a magician.'[20]

The Secret Doctrine Volume I explains, 'We see that every external motion, act, gesture, whether voluntary or mechanical, organic or mental, is produced and preceded by internal feeling or emotion, will or volition, and thought or mind. As no outward motion or change, when normal, in man's external body can take place unless provoked by an inward impulse, given through one of the three functions named, so with the external or manifested Universe.'[21]

This law is no longer a secret. Imagine life on our precious globe when it is put to use for selfless good. It is our responsibility as dedicated students of theosophy to work with compassion and in the best interests of all beings on our planet.

* * *

When asked 'What is theosophy?' I often include the term 'omnism'. Coined in the mid 19th Century, omnism describes the belief that all religions contain some of the truth, but no religion contains all of the truth. Similar wisdom is found in a quote attributed to the Persian poet Rumi, 'The truth was a mirror in the hands of God. It fell, and broke into pieces. Everybody took a piece of it, and they looked at it and thought they had the truth.'

Throughout history, humanity's selfishness, superstition, greed, ignorance and fear has only reinforced 'the greatest heresy': that we are separate from all other beings and things. The New Age/New Thought Movement of the last century was cherry picked from theosophical writings and ushered in the 'we are one' mentality but unfortunately, it also became a doctrine of separateness with many self-proclaimed gurus claiming that their way to oneness is the only way.

How truly wise is that archaic intelligence which left us this primary instruction: *man, know thyself and you will know the universe*. Through diligent and thorough self-reflection, self-examination, persistence and honesty we must look inside if we are ever to stand face to face with the truth within.

The spiritual journey is an arduous and painful one but we should remember that this life's loves and lessons are not lost. That which is important to our lower personality: status, wealth, validation from others means nothing to the formless, eternal soul. It makes no difference if we are a wealthy monarch with a titanic kingdom, what truly matters is what kind of person we were, how we treated others. Did we respect the environment and the animal kingdom? Were we selfish and cruel? Did we work to overcome our lower nature and leave this world a little better than when we arrived?

One does not have to have a near death experience (NDE) to understand the invaluable wisdom and insight such an experience can bring. Thanks to modern technology, most of us have the ability to document our lives on video and more near death experiences are being recorded and reported. It is no longer seen as taboo to share such truths and many are bravely coming forward with their stories from the 'other side' or 'inner side'. They return with a near verbatim description of the theosophical teachings.

There are firsthand accounts of vast, unconditional love, of compassion and understanding, of an overwhelming feeling of connection, oneness and unity. All this suffused with the knowledge that we are an unlimited expression of spirit becoming existence itself. In these NDEs the wisdom from past lives is recognised as is the importance of every person and situation in our current lives. All had a part to play and all are absolutely necessary.

Through the study and application of theosophy, we can begin to understand the wisdom brought back from NDEs. We start to see the bigger picture. We realise this current incarnation is just one moment in a physical shell with one earthly personality. We realise that our past lives offer insight as to why we behave the way we do. In the greater scheme of things, this lifetime is really just one 'day'. We begin to perceive the truth of things such as karmic connection, psychopathy, empathy, child prodigies, birthmarks, twins that are enemies or carbon copies, Tourettes, phobias, hearing voices, ghosts, dreams, extra sensory perception, UFOs, and why bad things happen to good people. These things start to make sense when we look beyond one lifetime to many lifetimes. Theosophy explains these things through reincarnation and our navigation of each earthly life becomes much more manageable.

The power is in our own hands. It cannot be doled out by clergy or guru. Of course the church would prefer that this knowledge be kept secret and exclusive, otherwise how would these institutions maintain healthy numbers of members, ensure their coffers remain full and maintain control over the hearts of mankind? True spiritual law always allows goodness and light to prevail. This light has come to illuminate the darkest, dusty corners of human greed, selfishness and lust for power.

Within all of us is a familiar, vociferous insistence that we must prove ourselves right. This voice is relentless, yet fragile, and takes offence easily. It judges, condemns, angers quickly, is envious and almost comically jealous of others, even people that are dear to us. It also fills us with self-doubt, tells us we are worthless, stupid, wrong but simultaneously reminds us that we are still special, separate and better than everyone else.

If we truly listen, we can start to recognise this voice as the voice of the egotistical lower self. It can be found inside each and every one of us. Let us acknowledge this voice with detachment and unconditional love and realise that although we hear it, it is entirely possible not to act upon what it says. This brutish inner speech has been called the ego and the false self. With practice it becomes easier to identify, and then its influence fades.

Meditation helps us enter the quiet space between our thoughts, to rise above the endless interior chatter of life in the physical world. When we look within, we discover the voice of the silence.

As the Buddhists say, 'Silence is not empty, it is full of answers.' This voice is our own built-in spiritual satnav. When we listen to it, we gain a sense of purpose, direction and great hope. Profound feelings of compassion arise. Then comes a clear call to action and a drive to get to work and serve. The time is now. 'Hast thou attuned thy being to Humanity's great pain, O candidate for light?'[22] 'Can there be bliss when all that lives must suffer? Shalt thou be saved and hear the whole world cry?'[23]

Theosophy is altruism, selflessness, compassion, kindness, unconditional love and understanding and service to all beings. Theosophy is to be applied in times of tragedy or triumph, fear or calm, certainty or doubt. Theosophy's teachings are put into practice by being kind to those who are unkind to us, by overcoming our need to be right, by realising that every opportunity or difficulty is a lesson and a test if we are willing to learn. Every action, no matter how small, can be inspired by the ancient, sacred teachings. It is our responsibility to become living theosophy.

Again, theosophy cannot be bought or taught,

but it can be earned and learned. Theosophy's truths are only words until put into action by mankind. You may have countless cookbooks. You can study them ad infinitum, but until you actually cook something, they remain only ink on a page. The same is true for theosophy. Unfortunately, far too many of us are focused on the books themselves and, more bizarrely, the personalities of those who wrote them. Life, itself, is our classroom. But unless we work to develop ourselves practically, we are simply indulging in 'mental masturbation'.

George Arundale writes, 'We have in the Theosophical Society today and outside the Theosophical Society people who insist that their particular truths or their particular theosophies are the only truths and the only theosophies. That is not only dangerous, but it is also untruthful. It means that the individual who insists upon his own particular way, upon his own particular interpretation of theosophy does not possess his way, does not possess his own particular theosophy, but is possessed by it, is obsessed by it, is enslaved by it.'[24]

I believe theosophical writings constitute a

textbook for humanity. The only things we truly have control over are our own thoughts, actions, responses, and occasionally our circumstances. We can make a powerful choice: to become the difference that helps alleviate the unnecessary suffering of all on our planet. The real meaning of life is for us to work tirelessly to conquer our own lower selves and leave our world a little better, a little brighter than when we came here. By doing this, we, like candles in the blackest night, help illuminate the darkness. 'To live to benefit mankind is the first step.'[25]

For theosophists, the number seven has a profound mystical significance. Below is a list of seven ideas that will help you apply theosophy in your daily life.

The Seven Cs of Theosophy

1. Carnal
2. Cause and Effect
3. Commonalities
4. Connection
5. Consciousness

6. Cosmos
7. Cycles

1. Carnal

A human being is a sevenfold being, extending far beyond the limits suggested by the five senses. Each person contains the vital life force, the astral body, the 'animal' or lower mind of man. Then there is the higher mind, the human soul that moves from life to life, next is the higher consciousness, the spiritual soul which serves as the instrument of the final principle. That final principle is the limitless ray of eternal, absolute consciousness.

2. Cause and Effect

Here we are talking about karma and reincarnation. Peace on earth is achievable when humanity understands the absolute law of equilibrium. Karma (balance) is not vengeful nor is it punishment from some supernatural being. It is simply the effects that result from the causes we have set in motion. The analogy of 'touching a hot stove' is often used because it is so accurate. Touch the stove and you will be burned. 'Do unto others as you'd have done to you' has been taught by sages through the ages as the 'golden rule'. Buddha compares karma to an echo or a shadow, 'As the echo belongs to the sound, and the shadow to the substance, so misery will overtake the evil-doer without fail.'

After a near death experience, many people return with a powerful understanding of the other person's point of view. They perceive the hurt they have caused through their actions and thoughts, both knowingly and unknowingly.

Life on earth is like going to school. If we do not learn the lessons, we will have to do them again. The Bhagavad Gita: 'There are two eternal paths: one light, the other dark. The first legs to liberation form the wheel of death and rebirth, the other path leads to this world again.'

We should choose to be kind and compassionate for its own sake, not because we hope for a reward.

3. Commonalities

All great teachers have said essentially the

same thing. Buddha, Krishna, Lao Tzu, Zarathustra, Jesus express similar truths but use different language and ideas. Their teachings are fundamentally theosophical. All beings recognise then sun as the ultimate source of life even though they give it many different names.

In 1839, the poet Phillip J. Bailey coined the term 'omnist' meaning the recognition and respect for all religions. An omnist acknowledges that all religions contain some of the truth but no one religion contains all of the truth. 'For it is only by studying the various great religions and philosophies of humanity, by comparing them dispassionately and with an unbiased mind, that men can hope to arrive at the truth.'[26]

4. Connection

We are told that 'all is one' but this concept is difficult to grasp and it can seem like an over-exaggeration. Everything originates from the causeless cause, the sourceless source. *The Secret Doctrine* describes the absolute as 'omnipresent, eternal, boundless, and immutable'. Edgar Mitchell, the sixth man to walk on the moon, upon looking back at the earth said, 'You develop an instant global consciousness, a people orientation, an intense dissatisfaction with the state of the world, and a compulsion to do something about it. From out there on the moon, international politics look so petty. You want to grab a politician by the scruff of the neck and drag him a quarter of a million miles out and say, *Look at that, you son of a bitch.*'[27]

Our earth is one of more than 7,000,000,000,000,000,000 (seven quintillion) planets in the known universe. The universe is unimaginably vast and ever expanding. Theosophy teaches that everything is an aspect of the same 'be-ness', from the atom to the universe and beyond. *The Voice of the Silence* warns us about the 'great dire heresy' of believing in our own separateness from all other beings and from the one universal, infinite self. Everything is one. How different life will be when all of us understand this eternal truth.

5. Consciousness

Know thyself, and thou shalt know the universe and God was one of three maxims inscribed at the entrance to the Temple of Apollo at Delphi. We need to look deep inside ourselves to find the eternal truth within and consciously unite with our own inner god. With humility and powerful unconditional love for all beings, we can come to understand that our consciousness is one and the same as that of the universe itself. 'I have said, Ye are gods; and all of you are children of the most High.' PSALMS 82:6. 'Know ye not that ye are Gods?' HERMETIC AXIOM.

6. Cosmos

The Sufi Mystic, Rumi, mellifluously reminds us: 'You are not a drop in the ocean, you are the entire ocean in a drop.'

'The Universe is worked and guided from within outwards. As above so it is below, as in heaven so on earth; and man - the microcosm and miniature copy of the macrocosm - is the living witness to this universal law and to the mode of its action.'[28]

The universe is the source of our consciousness, thoughts and intellect. Both man and the cosmos are septenary in nature and we share the same universal intelligence (divine thought) from which all of spirit, matter and mind originate. The cosmos is the ultimate 'nature' and nature is the true 'church'. You are the temple. You are where theosophy takes place. Everything is a reflection of you. It is all about you!

7. Cycles

The law of periodicity: 'This second assertion of the Secret Doctrine is the absolute universality of that law of periodicity, of flux and reflux, ebb and flow, which physical science has observed and recorded in all departments of nature... in it we see one of the absolutely fundamental laws of the universe.'[29]

Everything is evolving and renewing: day to night, breathing in and breathing out, birth to death to rebirth again, the rise and fall of the tides, the seasons - spring, summer, fall, winter - the waxing and waning of the moon, all of life is cycles within cycles. The law of activity and rest applies to all matter, to all living things and spirit, including the appearance and disappearance of worlds, universes and all of existence.

Our trials and tribulations are opportunities

for learning, and when life is calm and good, we get a much needed rest. Most importantly, we must remember that this cycle of renewal never ceases. It is the expectation that it will cease that causes us so much suffering. These cycles are not simply hellacious repetitions. They are stages of evolution, always moving forwards by no matter how small a degree. Pain is the usher of wisdom if we allow it to be.

Theosophy gives us every tool and paves the way for us all to understand our connection to each other. Let us unite as the cells of the endless, boundless being that we are. Together, in self-assessment, reflection and realignment, we can become the opposite of what still plagues mankind: selfishness, ignorance, superstition, fear, hate and greed. These are all causes of unnecessary suffering.

It is imperative that we bring the teachings of theosophy into education as soon as possible. We should make them accessible to children and young people, easy for them to comprehend, relevant and relatable. We cannot remain static. I believe H.P. Blavatsky would advocate the use of all the methods of communication available today. We must modernise the packaging and delivery of these timeless teachings and work together selflessly to share them far and wide. It is also imperative we stop worshipping and idolising the people who wrote down the texts, including Blavatsky herself.

There is a solution to be found in every problem. Painful situations continue until the lessons are learned. I am not here to offer an academic study of theosophy's teachings, I simply wish to share how I use theosophy in my daily life. One can study, memorise and reiterate the ageless wisdom but it is all for naught unless the teachings are applied in every aspect of our daily lives. Theosophy is a way of living, a way of being, and it can be of use in every aspect of life. By choosing this way of living, we not only benefit from our experience but we pave the way to a better life, for ourselves and those around us. The 'great battle' takes place between 'good' and 'evil' but not via exterior forces nor by independent supernatural beings in some other realm. This battle occurs within each of us between our higher and lower selves. Every victorious step forwards aids the healing of our planet as we work in harmony with nature. By recognising our true selves and realigning ourselves with responsibility, compassion, understanding and love, our efforts help to ease the unnecessary suffering of all beings on earth.

'Mind, heart, brain, all are obscure and dark until the first great battle has been won. Be not appalled and terrified by this sight; keep your eyes fixed on the small light and it will grow.'[30]

Nature is the true church. You are the temple. Theosophy is all about you.

'Then from the heart that power shall rise into the sixth, the middle region, the place between thine eyes, when it becomes the breath of the ONE-SOUL, the voice which filleth all..

'Tis only then thou canst become a 'Walker of the Sky'…'[31]

NOTES

1. George Arundale, *Theosophy and Truth*, Theosophical Publishing House, 1900s.

2. Ibid.

3. Helena Petrovna Blavatsky, *The Key to Theosophy*, Theosophical Publishing Company, 1889.

4. Helena Petrovna Blavatsky, *Chelas and Ley Chelas*, The Theosophist, vol VI, no. 1, October 1884.

5. Helena Petrovna Blavatsky, *Collected Writings vol IX*, Theosophical Publishing House, 1962.

6. Helena Petrovna Blavatsky, *The Key to Theosophy*, Theosophical Publishing Company, 1889.

7. Helena Petrovna Blavatsky, *Collected Writings vol XII*, Theosophical Publishing House, 1973.

8. William Walker Atkinson aka Yogi Ramacharaka, *The Fourteen Lessons in Yogi Philosophy and Oriental Occultism*, Yogi Publication Society, 1903.

9. Usually attributed to Helena Petrovna Blavatsky but the source is unverified.

10. Ibid.

11. Helena Petrovna Blavatsky, *The Secret Doctrine vol I*, Theosophical Publishing Company, London,1888.

12. Ibid.

13. Ibid.

14. Helena Petrovna Blavatsky, *The Key to Theosophy*, Theosophical Publishing Company, 1889.

15. Helena Petrovna Blavatsky, *The Secret Doctrine vol I*, Theosophical Publishing Company, London,1888.

16. Helena Petrovna Blavatsky, *The Theosophical Glossary*, The Theosophical Publishing Society, 1892.

17. Raghavan Iyer, *Kriyashakti*, Hermes Magazine, August 1984.

18. Helena Petrovna Blavatsky, *Collected Writings vol XI*, Quest Books, 1966.

19. The Three Initiates (William Walker Atkinson, Anna Kingsford and Edward Maitland), *The Kybalion*, The Yogi Publication Society, 1908.

20. Helena Petrovna Blavatsky, *Isis Unveiled*, J. W. Bouton, 1877.

21. Helena Petrovna Blavatsky, *The Secret Doctrine vol I*, Theosophical Publishing Company, London,1888.

22. Helena Petrovna Blavatsky, *The Voice of the Silence*, Theosophical Publishing Company, London, 1889.

23. Ibid.

NOTES

24. George Arundale, *Theosophy and Truth*,
    Theosophical Publishing House, 1900s.

25. Helena Petrovna Blavatsky, *The Voice of the Silence*,
    Theosophical Publishing Company, London, 1889.

26. Helena Petrovna Blavatsky, *The Key to Theosophy*,
    Theosophical Publishing Company, 1889.

27. Attributed to Edgar D. Mitchell, Apollo 14 astronaut.

28. Helena Petrovna Blavatsky, *The Secret Doctrine vol I*,
    Theosophical Publishing Company, London, 1888.

29. Ibid.

30. Mabel Collins, *Light on the Path*, George Redway, London, 1888.

31. Helena Petrovna Blavatsky, *The Voice of the Silence*,
    Theosophical Publishing Company, London, 1889.

George Arundale

George Sydney Arundale was born on 1 December 1878 in Surrey, England.

He was raised by his aunt, Francesca Arundale who often hosted H. P. Blavatsky at her home in London. George became a member of the Theosophical Society in England in 1895 and joined the London Lodge.

He was tutored by C. W. Leadbeater and in 1900 he graduated from St John's College, Cambridge.

In 1897, he went to India with his aunt to become Professor of History and English at the Central Hindu College, Benares. Being found unfit for active service in World War I, he returned to in 1916, and supported Annie Besant in the Home Rule for India campaign.

In 1920, he married Srimati Rukmini Devi, who was from a theosophical Brahmin family. She accompanied him on his worldwide lecture tours, and became well known to theosophists in many countries.

He became General Secretary of the Theosophical Society in Australia in 1926, where, in addition to his theosophical duties, he undertook humanitarian and political work. He also became Regionary Bishop of the Liberal Catholic Church in India.

In 1927 he conducted a lengthy lecture tour in Europe and the United States. He undertook similar lecture tours each year from 1931 to 1934.

Arundale was elected International President of The Theosophical Society in 1933 and, from 1934, developed a seven year plan which included the development of Adyar, and ensuring the solidarity of the society.

He introduced two new publications. The International Theosophical Year Book was issued annually from 1937 to 1942. The Theosophical World, which changed title to The Theosophical Worker in 1939, was a monthly members newsletter published from 1936 to 1946.

He was diabetic and from 1942 his health began to deteriorate. He died on 12 August 1945.

Theosophy and Truth
by George Arundale (19??)

The two great pillars upon which the structure of The Theosophical Society rests are its three great Objects and its unique Motto - 'There is no religion higher than Truth.' The first Object is, of course, supreme - the formation of a nucleus, a concentration, of the existing Universal Brotherhood of Humanity. All who desire to join The Theosophical Society must be welcome so to do, whoever they are, provided it is their desire to lead a brotherly life. Otherwise it would be impossible for them to be constituent parts of a nucleus designed to this end. But they should also be in sympathy with the two Objects which, as they are pursued, lead to a deeper realization of the fact of Universal Brotherhood. Members of The Theosophical Society are people who have a real and practical sympathy for Brotherhood, but who also have sympathy both with the study of religion, philosophy and science to the further elucidation of Brotherhood, and with the exploration of the as yet undiscovered, no less to the further elucidation of Brotherhood. In such study and exploration they may be disinclined to engage. Yet it is vital study and exploration, and demands the sympathetic appreciation of all members, no matter what their personal relationship to it may be.

What Is Truth ?

It seems to me, however, that while the Objects of The Society are in the forefront of the Theosophical consciousness of each one of us, we are apt to forget that our motto is a no less fundamental part of the structure of our Society. In it we exalt Truth, without defining Truth, above all forms of Truth. The Sanskrit word *Sat* is well translated as Truth. But we proceed to translate the word *Dharma* as religion, and say that there is no religion higher than Truth. 1 think that this translation quite wrongly narrows the whole conception sought to be conveyed in the motto. I have always understood that the word 'Dharma' signifies right adjustment between the individual and his surroundings, right relationship; or possibly in a general way 'righteousness'. But it certainly does not mean that which we ordinarily understand by the word 'religion'. There is no righteousness higher than Truth. There is no expression of Life higher than Truth. These would, 1 am inclined to think, be more accurate translations of the motto of the Maharajahs of Benares than the translation we normally employ. Surely there is no religion higher than Truth. But equally there is no philosophy higher than Truth. There is no Art higher than Truth. There is no Science higher than Truth.

And even then the nature of the Truth must needs vary with the stage of evolution of the individual life. There is no righteousness for any individual higher than his fullest expression of Truth, than the fullest expression possible to him at his evolutionary level. Such righteousness will doubtless be expressed in terms of religion, but no less will it be expressed in many other terms, according to individual temperament.

The Relativity of Truth

Therefore, Truth is relative to each circumstance and condition of Life. 1 think we are almost entitled to say that one man's truth may be another man's falsehood, though I am not sure that we have any right to use the word 'falsehood' at all. In any ease we can say that what is true for one may not necessarily be true for another, and that what may be supremely true for one may have little or no place among the verities of another. It is impossible to envisage absolute Truth, for parts do not contain the whole of which they are parts. Yet inasmuch as every part is in some measure a reflection of its whole, is consubstantial with its whole, Truth absolute is implied in it, is latent in it though not patent in it.

Thus is it that I conceive of our Science of Theosophy as a very special mode of the Truth absolute, and of The Theosophical Society as a Movement embodying the search for Truth. As The Theosophical Society stands before the world, there is certainly no commitment to what we call Theosophy. No member is in any way under the slightest obligation to study, still less to accept, Theosophy. There is no Object such as might be expressed in the words: 'To study the Science of Theosophy'. There is a definite commitment to Brotherhood. There is a definite commitment to the study of religion, philosophy and science, and to the exploration of the undiscovered, at all events for those who feel so inclined. But the fact that The Society is called The Theosophical Society cannot surely be held to imply the obligation for every member to study Theosophy. Obviously, the majority of the members are likely to be students of Theosophy. But the first Object of The Society is not to study Theosophy, but to form a nucleus of the Universal Brotherhood of Humanity, which surely means that it may well be composed of many people who will not be concerning themselves with Theosophy as most of us know the Science. A nucleus of the Universal Brotherhood cannot be limited to a handful of students of Theosophy.

Where Theosophy Enters

On the other hand, it is deeply significant that Theosophy and The Theosophical Society are twins. They were reborn together in 1875, and have been growing up in beauty side by side ever since. There must be some very intimate relationship between Theosophy and The Theosophical Society, or they would not have been reborn at the same time and to the same people. Personally, I feel that Brotherhood matters more than aught else, and that it is clothed in no exclusive form, nor is there but a single way to its achievement. l can well conceive of an individual joining our Society and yet denying the value of the Science of Theosophy to himself, though in no way denying its possible value to others. Where, then, does Theosophy enter? It enters, I think, as a suggestion relative to the possible bases of Truth which is more, of Truth which is at the ultimate root of all Truths, of Truth which is, if I may be pardoned the phrase, relatively absolute. It enters as a statement of the Greatest Common Measure of all faiths, of all philosophies, of all sciences, and of that beyond of which religions, philosophies and sciences are time-projections in this outer world. It enters as a bird's-eye view of the evolutionary process as seen by those who have acquired the wings of spirituality. It enters as witness to the Love and the Justice and the Purpose of God amidst all the seeming negations and futilities of His beneficence. Theosophy is suggested to be a Wisdom even more ancient than the religions, even though it appears to us today with a Greek label. In Hinduism it is known as Brahmavidya - the Wisdom of the Supreme Being. It is declared to be the eternal river whence the irrigating wells visible to man derive their fructifying waters.

Theosophy No Dogma

Theosophy is no dogma. It is no formal religion. It is no specific mode of science. It is no carefully constructed philosophy representing the gaze of man into the heavens. It is an Experience of Reality on the part of some who, transcending the microcosm, have become in a measure free in the macrocosm, and describe something of their vision of the infinite as reflected in, and in terms of, the finite. In our classic literature we may read of the vision, of the experience, but without obligation, without an iota of penalty for doubt, or even for unbelief. 'Thus have we seen', say some great knowers of the Wisdom. Those who are eager to see will be inspired by the vision of others, be it but to see differently - whenever and wherever a human, still more a superhuman, soul cries out: 'I see! I see!' let others look, so that they too may see, even though otherwise. Some have seen that which we sum up in the word 'Theosophy'. Some have seen that which they sum up otherwise, in other words. It matters more to see than to believe. It matters more to see than to hope. It matters more to see than to follow. It matters more to see even than to know. Let those whose eyes are opening look when they hear the cry: 'I see.'

Yet Truth is more than any picture of it, than any form of it, than any description of it. Far be it from any of us, save, perchance, for ourselves, to insist that Truth is here or there, in such and such a book, in such and such a person, alone, or in supreme degree. For ourselves any book, any teacher, any well of Life, may be the exclusive giver of the Truth we momentarily need and are able to assimilate. But we cannot deny to others that freedom to seek and to find Truth which has enabled us, seeking, to find. Truth is more than the Theosophy we Theosophists know and cherish. Is not Truth everywhere, as well as in our own individual conceptions, which we so readily insist comprise the Truth, the whole Truth, and nothing but the Truth ?

Truths Change

Truths change in form at all events as we ourselves must change. Today such and such a book reflects for us Truth's peaks. A Scripture, a philosophical dissertation; for Theosophists, perhaps, *The Secret Doctrine* or *At the Feet of the Master*, or some other classical work. But we shall not forever be reading the book which in this incarnation represents for us the highest revelation. We shall not be carrying under our arms the volumes of *The Secret Doctrine* as we pass through the valley of death into the hills of heaven, and thence back again on to the plains of earth. It is not the book that matters, nor even the teacher, nor yet the tradition, but the Life. And the Life must reveal itself in form after form, in book after book, in teacher after teacher, in tradition after tradition, until the kaleidoscopically changing forms reveal the constant and unchanging Life. In varied forms shall we be seeking Truth, until we become able to perceive Truth in all forms. Time after time shall we be saying that Truth is here, and here, and here, not there, nor there, nor there, until we discover that Truth is everywhere, until we identify Truth with all that lives, until we perceive Truth treading wonderfully and mysteriously her gorgeous way in a myriad differing forms.

We Theosophists are seekers after Truth, even though we are also, like the rest of the world, finders of Truth. We rejoice in the Truth we have found, but are restless to move onwards to Truth which we have not yet found. Each of our Objects is dynamic in that it represents seeking after more than it represents finding. Away from the Truth which enslaves us, away from the Truth we have conquered, to the Truth which may have yet to enslave us, to the Truth we have yet to conquer! The Theosophy we have must not enslave us, nor must we rest content in its conquest. It is but the thin edge of endless Truth.

The Universality of Truth

I have been much preoccupied in my spare moments by the thought of the motto of The Theosophical Society: 'There is no religion higher than Truth'. What is this truth than which no religion is higher? To what extent do we possess it? What truth remains, and how are we to seek it? We pay far too little attention to the motto of The Theosophical Society, for if we were to pay more attention to it we should have a clearer conception as to the nature of truth, and having that clearer conception, we should be much more understanding, less dogmatic, less aggressive, less denunciatory than so many of us are with regard to a particular reflection of truth which we imagine we perceive.

It is extremely difficult to define truth adequately. One of the most useful definitions of truth is the definition which relates it to its effect upon human character. An individual should be known by his truths; in other words, he should be profoundly affected by that which he regards as truth; it should deeply influence his life down here, and should in fact be his guiding star, the light on his path. 1 believe that truth can be as well defined by the character of the individual it produces as in any other way, for if we strive to define truth in any other way, we are practically confronted with the fact that truth is co-existent with life. There is no truth but life. 1 do not think we can go any further than that. Even if we think of the Theosophy so far disclosed to us in terms of its laws, and so forth, all these are aspects, functions, expressions of life, nothing more than that.

The question then arises as to what is an individual's relation to what we call truth? How is he to seek it? How is he to discover it? How is he to use it when he has it?

Everyone Has His Truth

Now the more I brood upon the whole question of truth, the more I am perfectly convinced that each individual has his own truth, however different it may be or even apparently contradictory to the truths of others. No individual is without life; therefore, no individual is without truth. While it may be said in the case of some that they are more full of life and therefore more full of truth than others, for the most part we have the truth we need for the lives we lead. I, therefore, take a very catholic view of truth so as to accord truth to everyone, being sure that no one is without truth to the measure of the standard of his stage of evolution. If he has not one truth he has another truth. If he does not possess truths which we ourselves cherish exceedingly, and which we regard as the very essence and heart of truth, he has other truth no less vital in fact to him, no less the heart of truth, so far as he is concerned, than that which to us seems so extremely true.

Since, therefore, no one is without truth - for everyone is in possession of it since he is in possession of life - the utmost that is incumbent upon us is to declare it, not to use it as a weapon, not to use it so as to confront other so-called lesser truths and to hold them up as being inferior, but to declare what we have and let the declaration work its own way. I think we have as much the duty to declare the truths that are ours as we have the duty to live. It is surely our duty to live as fully, as richly, as strongly, as forthgoingly, as we possibly can. That should involve the expression of the very essence of that truth, of that life, namely the truths we hold.

The Power of the Truth

If there is to be any acid test as to the value of any particular truth to the individual, if he is to challenge himself on the question as to whether he has the truth which should be most to him - so that there is nothing more for the time being which could mean more than the truth he already possesses - then he might very well look to see the influence and effect the truths he holds have upon the life he leads, upon his character, his understanding, his power to recognize and perceive the truths dwelling in other people. Hence, while from one point of view, each person has his own separate and individual and uniquely different truth, from another point of view he must so hold even those truths which are unique to him that he is able to perceive with joy the truths which are unique to other people. It may be true that he knows he has a truth which would mean much to other people if they possessed it.

We Theosophists, for example, may feel clear that we have in Theosophy life, truth, which the majority of the world does not possess; hence, the certainly urgent need for declaring Theosophy. On the other hand there are many in the outer world who possess that which we do not possess. While we may say that we have this, that and the other truth, they may have this, that and the other truth which perhaps we may possess in less degree, or not possess at all. You may say that is a rather negative condition of being. What is the worthwhileness of being a Theosophist if you cannot feel that the world is needing something urgently that we have and is the poorer without it? I definitely feel that we have the duty of declaring, and with emphasis, strength and eagerness to convince, the truths we possess, that we believe to be ours. But we have no call to be denunciatory, to compare our truths with other people's truths to the detriment of other people's truths; we have no cause to place ourselves on pedestals of superiority as if we had something so very special that we are far in front of other people who do not possess the specialities in which we rejoice.

Theosophy and Truth

I do not think it is possible for The Theosophical Society to fulfil its First Object and to establish a real nucleus of Universal Brotherhood if we confine ourselves to Theosophy in the sense in which we use the term at the present time. Theosophy is of course a specific aspect of science, it is a specific interpretation of life, it is an emphasis on certain truths. That is what Theosophy is, as we have it. From one point of view it is the ancient and eternal Wisdom and is all-inclusive, but there are not many Theosophists who have that Theosophy. Rather have they the specialized Theosophy which deals with special laws, planes of consciousness, which deals with races, rounds, and all the other teachings set forth in our classic literature. That is the average Theosophist's grasp. How many Theosophists have the universal, eternal and all-inclusive wisdom which Theosophy essentially is? Each one of us has a reflection but not the White Light as a whole.

In these circumstances, therefore, I think we ought to realize that we have, when we are thinking of this Theosophy of ours, truth only in part. More and more, as I brood upon these things, do I become convinced that while it is true that this particular aspect of wisdom we call Theosophy is ours with which to permeate the whole world, yet there are other aspects. If there is no religion higher than truth and if each individual has his own truth, we need that truth, such as he has, in order to perfect our nucleus of the Universal Brotherhood of humanity. I feel, therefore, that while on the one hand it is our business to emphasize the Theosophy handed down to us by the Elder Brethren through our great leaders, we must not forget that Universal Brotherhood is perhaps more than the Theosophy that we know, this specialized form of Theosophy. I do not say for a moment that Universal Brotherhood is more than Theosophy. No! But it is more than the Theosophy that the average individual calls by that name. Speaking as President of The Theosophical Society, I feel that my work largely, not entirely but largely, is to make our membership as inclusive as it possibly can be made, so that we may be enriched by innumerable differences and not starved by the lack of them.

Facets of the Diamond of Truth

In the beginning was a particular word, a special word, and that special and particular word was with H.P. Blavatsky and in fact was H.P. Blavatsky. But that word is not the only word, nor was it pronounced in those early days in the only way it could be pronounced. There are surely other pronunciations as certainly as there are other words, and if only we could as to our Society become collectors of, includers, of differences, on certain terms, our Society would be very very much the stronger, without in any way detracting from the fact that we have a special restoration of truth which goes under the name of Theosophy and which has its own particular definitions. When I say 'on terms', I mean that we must be mutually appreciative of each other's truths no matter how widely divergent one truth is from another. What should mark off The Theosophical Society from all other movements should be this wealth of differences mutually appreciated and understood, without there being as between one and another even the minutest depreciation, still less of course, the spirit of antagonism. I feel that very strongly.

I do not think that it matters that we differ. But I think it does matter how we differ. We have to begin to learn to differ in a spirit of harmony and to go our different ways, however radically different one way may be from another, in a spirit of appreciation of the way in which somebody else is going his way.

Discover for Yourself

That brings me to a point which in some way is related to this fact that each individual has his own truth, namely, that he should be careful not to borrow truth but to discover it. Very many people borrow truths. They have their truths on loan and so it often happens that an individual who has a truth on loan finds that it does not satisfy him when put to some great test or when he happens to be in some great need. I think that The Theosophical Society is in the stage in which we must lay stress on each individual very definitely going his own way, a way he must learn to tread without antagonism, condemnation, denunciation of other people, full of joy as to his own way and full of respect as to the ways of others.

Each one of us ought to take advantage of all the truth that we see around us. We ought to take advantage of each other's truths which each one of us is more or less living day by day, not in order to copy but in order to understand, so that light may be thrown on one's own way thereby. I am afraid that during many years very many of us, and very many even of our leaders, have held their truths almost like bludgeons. To me, if there is any negation of truth whatever, it is when that truth is held as a weapon of attack on somebody else's beliefs, no matter how crude they may seem to the wielder of the weapon. We have in The Theosophical Society today and outside The

Theosophical Society people who insist that their particular truths or their particular Theosophies are the only truths and the only Theosophies. That is not only dangerous, but it is almost untruthful. It means that the individual who insists upon his own particular way, upon his own particular interpretation of Theosophy does not possess his way, does not possess his own particular Theosophy, but is possessed by it, is obsessed by it, is enslaved by it.

Truth Is Dynamic

I can conceive that an individual must go into the world as a slave to his truths so that he may fulfil certain purposes, riding rough-shod over the truths of others, but such circumstances must indeed be rare. It is perfectly clear, to me at all events, that we have to understand and appreciate, to cause the truths of others to shine upon our way to illumine its course more clearly. For wherever you are, be it in Theosophy or in science, or in any department of life - religion, politics - there is always change, and truth which is less is constantly giving way to truth which is more; so that the truth which is less practically swings into the background, and the truth which is more occupies just for the time being the foreground, until it in its turn must swing into the background and other truth takes its place, because truth is dynamic, truth is movement, truth is growth. There is nothing static about any truth which anyone holds. No one holds any truth in form forever, nor even in life for the matter of that. Your most cherished opinion, the truths which you hold most dear, the truths which are nearest to you, which mean most to you, which give you the courage and the hope and the peace and joy you need, all of them are far less than that into which they are destined to grow, are but shadows of the light to come.

Thus is it that one holds one's truths lightly. One does not clutch them as if one never wanted to let them go again. One holds them lightly, uses them while they are usable, and then allows them to go below the threshold of the waking consciousness into the storehouse of experience. The Theosophy that you and I know, about which we talk perhaps with such certainty and clarity and definiteness, is but the shadow of the Theosophy that we shall know. Not only that, but the Theosophy which seems to us such abundant life, with all the truths which we have in our conventional Theosophy - that is only one facet of the great diamond of Theosophy. The time will come when we shall turn from that facet to another facet which in its turn may appear to exclude those constituent elements which mean so much, in fact mean everything, to us in the facet turned towards us in this particular life.

Theosophy Only a Fragment

So many people are anxious that they shall continue the next life more or less in the same way in which they have been following this life. They hope they will come back into this Theosophy, into The Theosophical Society, into contact again with such and such leaders, as early as possible know in their next lives the things which they came to know in later years in this life; they are so anxious to repeat the same thing over and over again. That shows sometimes that we are holding these truths far too closely to us, we are hugging them as if someone were endeavouring to steal them from us. If you think of just the little bit of Theosophy we know, it is but the smallest fragment of the Eternal Wisdom of life, and for my own part, rather than repeat next life the particular truths which have been satisfactory to me in this life, I should like a complete change, l should like the kaleidoscope of my life to be shaken so vigorously that a picture appears entirely different from the picture which the original shaking brought to view in the beginning of the life which I am now leading.

Truth Is Everywhere

I can think, even as I am talking to you now, of a life radically different from this one without most of the beliefs and truths which certainly are very dear to me now, and which I hope I shall have forever, but which I shall be quite glad to see temporarily obscured for the sake of other truths which these truths themselves may now be obscuring. Well, that is another matter, and in the meantime I hope that I myself, and I hope every Theosophist, may increasingly have the power to perceive truth everywhere and not exclusively anywhere. After all, truth is everywhere, life is everywhere, and to discover, truth in everything is to begin to understand and to know life.

It seems to me that our work is largely to be free, and I do not think you are free unless you can dwell everywhere in a spirit of freedom, unless you can dwell in every faith, in every human condition of life, in innumerable antitheses and be perfectly and beautifully and happily at home. We must be able to dwell in antitheses, in forms, ceremonies, restrictions, at home, free, kings in them, because there is no frontier to our power to move about. I have a feeling that an individual who says, 'I do not care about ceremonies' is an individual who is not free. I feel that an individual who says, 'I am not interested in religion' is an individual who is not free. An individual who says, 'I prefer this country to that, this nation to that nation' is not free, he is imprisoned. Life is universal, be it a form, a ceremony, a faith, a nation, an individual. No matter in what form, there is life, there is God, there is a growth, there is truth, and a Theosophist, a lover of the Universal Wisdom, should be able to be free in all these modes of truth's and life's manifestation. I think we have to learn so to be and not to be negative in our declarations of truth, saying, 'It is not here, it is not there, it is not elsewhere.' We must be positive in our declaration of truth, saying, 'It is everywhere.'

From Slavery to Kingship

The great search of the Theosophist is the discovery of truth everywhere and the exalting of truth everywhere. There is no greater service that any individual can render to any other individual than to cause that individual to feel an exaltation, an exultation, with regard to those truths which are nearest and dearest to him. If we are really Theosophists, it seems to me that we can do no better than to take each individual where he is and to try to exalt him where he is, try to help him to exult more wisely where he is. It is not very easy, because in many many cases you are confronted with an individual who is in a condition of dogmatism narrow in its rigid exclusiveness, or of despair helpless in its utter hopelessness. I do not say that it is not a necessary stage of evolution to be certain you are right and that everybody else is wrong. Yet in fact nobody is much more right than anybody else. It is the habit of the individual who is very full of his temporary self to be sure that he is right, that his views are right, that his scheme, his plan of life is right. Those individuals are a little difficult because they have so great a hold on time that they have nothing wherewith to take hold of eternity, and that is their weakness. They live in the prisons of their own temporary narrownesses and they are very sure, self-satisfied, self-opinionated. They are not free. While, of course, it is true that an individual must be a slave before he can be a king, a Theosophist should be on the watch that the period of slavery be passed as quickly as possible, that his face be turned as early as possible towards his kingship.

The Rainbow

To conclude, I feel that we have to enter into this third period of The Society's life, a period of recognition of the universality of truth, and of the need to have that universality as perfectly expressed within the confines of our Society as is possible, so that even the apparently most emphatic contradictions may learn within The Society to live harmoniously and constructively at peace. Thus do we move away from external authority to internal authority, from external forms to individuality, from all that is without to the within, so that valuing as perhaps we have not valued our own within, we may not seek to make it a weapon wherewith to try to mould other withins to the forms of ours, but to make it a means whereby we appreciate the within of each, the individuality of each, and through our own eagerness to develop our own individuality, become able to encourage others to develop their individualities not along our lines but along theirs. So may every colour of the rainbow clearly be expressed, with the result that a White Light becomes beautifully manifested in all its exquisite whiteness by very reason of its constituent colours.